# Poems for Every - a Compilation

## Contents

Book 1 - Just Some Poems for Everyday People

Book 2 - Just Some More Poems for Everyday People

Book 3 - Further Poems for Everyday People

"Words can paint a thousand pictures"

©Jon Palmer January 2017

# Just Some Poems for Everyday People

## Book 1

Jon Palmer

# For Gary and big bros everywhere

© 2016 Jon Palmer

## **Sit here a while**

Autumn turns reds and browns, mist upon both grass and crowns,
and damper turns the air.

In this change, emotions rage of love and fun and care.


And when winter bites and frosts they smite,
and boughs lay gnarled and bare.

In that chill, I'm close to you, come walk or touch or stare.


And in spring, buds grew with colourful hue
and the oak it greens and spreads.

In that surge, feelings merge, laughter and tears are wed.


Now bright summer haze with glowing glaze,
the fruits bear nature's style.

And in that warmth, I think of you, just pause here for a while.


What was now has become what was then, the same is gone forever.
But what magical memories of halcyon days of shared fun and joint endeavour.

So through the changing moods of each turning month
when I stop and think of thee,
please come and sit a while, and smile along with me.

# **Sommenambulism**

I live the trench, I breathe the trench, the trench has become my soul;

I stand here a shadow in a dark, damp hole.

No road forward, no pathway back, directionless, hopelessness, lost;

into tumultuous evil, men such as I are tossed.

To the glorious youth, such miserable ends;

for in the mud, lionhearts lay.

The slaying of a generation;

day after day after day.

Just lads, just our lads, from field and from farm;

stolen from the plough, taken from the calm.

Lads, just our lads, from city and from town;

lured from the factory to face machine gun down.

Accept orders, touch death, go over the top;

devastation, chaos, scythe the flowering crop!

Don't look for reasons, blame it on fate;

stand with your 'pals', fall with your mates!

Now let time return placidity for friends and for foes;

rest, just rest boys, in your neat, tended rows.

Years may have distanced us, a whole century has passed;

yet our respect remains undiminished, find peace lads, at last.

## A South-West View

I cannot say

why I walk this way

and tread upon such turf.

I cannot say

why I walk this way

to gaze upon its surf.

This clifftop view,

sea's changing hue,

now what can that be worth?

I cannot say,

for there is no way

to put a price on mirth.

# Today the Words are Hiding

Today the words are hiding,
entangled by my mind.

Today the words are hiding,
may tomorrow them I find.

I search, I strive; paralysis.
For completely do I stall.

When I need the words of kings,
I find only those of fools.

Today the words are hiding,
entombed within my mind.

Today the words are hiding,
May tomorrow them I find.

# The Demise of the Dodo

Oh what did the dodo, do do

to end up gone forever?

I'll tell you what the dodo did do

and it wasn't very clever.

She laid her eggs on the ground you see,

instead of safe up in a great big tree.

And when sailors arrived with cats with claws,

she still laid her eggs in the grass on the floor.

They got broken and eaten and never did grow.

And that's what the dodo did do, you know

.........and it wasn't very clever.

# Autumn

Time transcended into colour, lights every branch and limb

Time flamed into colour, autumn held within

                Like the tide of the sea,

                              so remorselessly,

churns the clock,

        turns the changes in

**Avebury**

Monoliths standing vast through the ages;

resisters of time and all of its rages.

Watching, listening, sensing; permanence.

Guardians from the ancients; spiritual ambience.

Magical, earthly, devoid of pretence;

stand on forever, be forever immense.

## Good Old Cuppa

The only solution to a crises anew,

is to whack on the kettle and put on a brew.


## A Cornish Feast

When you're ravenous and need food fasty,

nothing compares to a Cornish pasty.


## The Cuddly

Some men are tough yet remain unready,

to part at all from their childhood teddy.


## It's Going to Cost ya

I like my Coffee, I love my latté.

I take it skinny, I aint no fatté.

# **The Olympics**

The Olympic Games, a human story

of speed, strength, skill; of pain and glory.

Is this their day? Is it now or never?

Can victory reward endeavour?


The crowd gathered, enthralled, packed so dense;

living the action, engrossed, intense.

The air, it crackles, fizzes, buzzes....and ignites.

The hum, the throng, such sounds, such sights.

As all plays out on the stage below,

emotions ebb and feelings flow.


And within that cauldron, fate unfolds.

Faster, higher, stronger, ....gold, gold, gold!

## **Me Bike**

Give me my bike and the wind in my face,

the power of cog and leg driven pace.


Let me ride amid the village, the street and the town,

struggle up hill and speed back down.


I want to feel the landscape and live that air,

cycle with freedom, pedal without care.


Give me my bike and the wind in my face,

an enormous smile and leg driven pace.

# **Time**

Time, they said, will fly by;

that you can't hold it in your hand.

Time, they said, just passes,

through fingers, just like sand.

But not for me, it will not!

Not for me, so cruel.

Time for me will move slowly.

I would defy the rule!

But time for me moves quickly,

despite my given best.

Rapid how it disappears,

as it does for all the rest.

Ticking relentlessly onwards; how I've gripped that minute hand,

closed my fingers tightly together, to halt that falling sand.

Oh time and tide relentless, no matter whom you be.

Time it slips so effortlessly and it does not wait for me.

# **The Downs**

Rolling fields of green and gold;

framed by the hedgerows that binds them bold.


Sounds abound and dance and thrill;

melodic streams, blackbirds' trill.


And looming behind, a dark brooding sky;

is there anywhere better? No say I!

# The Majestic Oak

Graceful silhouette against the grey, leaden blandness;

twisting, weaving, intricate, and wondrous.

Robustly filling that colourless frame;

tirelessly confronting the frosts and the rains.

Changing, adapting; a growing, living tale.

How majestic the oak! To your grandeur we hail!

## Out We Stride

Come with me as out we stride
through morning mist, betwixt taxi ride.

Through the red bricked streets, victorian rows,
where life has ebbed and life still flows.

By flats and semis and corner caffs,
Mansion homes and maladious gaffs.

Come with me as out we stride,
through morning mist, betwixt taxi ride.

Look into all those unfamiliar faces;
young faces, old faces, friendly faces,
knife-etched faces,
that tell a tale of a thousand places.

Caring minds, selfish minds,
sharp minds, addled minds,
step into the thoughts of a thousand kinds,
of yellowed fingers or jaundiced thinking,
of fading flowers and hypocrisy stinking,
of the meddler, the peddler, the wearied soul lost,
silently screaming, "Please give a toss."

Of doting mums and losers in the bookies,
of the seasoned old-timers and wide-eyed rookies,
of tarnished dreams and love letters tainted,
of the takers and the haters and of the truly sainted,
of those who see beauty where none should exist,
of those people of reason and those quick to the fist.

Come with me as out we stride
through morning mist, betwixt taxi ride.

Dare you look? Or do you hide?
As into the mourning streets we stride.

# **Dreamtime**

Don't stop the child from dreaming;
please try not to pre-empt a fall.
For without that child dreaming,
this world is bland and cruel.

Don't stop the child from believing,
even when life is not all it seems.
For we are a shell and are empty,
if our children cannot dream.

## The Brown Jug

The rugger is on and England I cheer.
I'm out with my mates and a pint of good beer.

The scores are level, two tries a piece;
                         such pressure on the kickers.
I'm watching it on the television;
                         it's too dear to go to Twickers!


## Dedication

Too much pizza, too many pies,
burgers, kebabs, hot dogs and fries.
Years of slobbery, decades of telly;
goodness me, how I've earned this belly!

## **Hair Today, Gone Tomorrow**

Before they laugh at me and harsh words get said,
should I buy a hair-piece to cover-up my head?

You see, I can't escape the reality, I am going bald.
Will a wig, really work? Will anyone be fooled!

Perhaps I should try a comb-over, try 'doing a Bobby'?
But that will stick-up in the wind or even go floppy.

I could try magic shampoo but truly I doubt
that this would make my hair follicles sprout.

Hmmmm, a transplant would work but would make me real glum
if I thought that those hairs had come from my bum!

Oh, how I hate and detest that hairless spot!
Sod you all, I'll shave off the lot!




## **C'Mon You Reds!**

I should be used to the disappointment, really I oughta;
I guess it's the burden of each Swindon supporter.

# **A Day at the Races**

Horses for courses, runners and riders;
back the favourite or try the outsiders.

Horses for courses, runners and riders;
have a pork roll and plenty of ciders.

Study the form, or just pick a name;
going is soft, horse has gone lame.

Feeling more lucky, it's time for a win;
look at those odds, we must be quids in.

Under starter's orders, crack of the whip,
an early leader, what a great tip!

One furlong to go, the race is still led;
photo finish, lost by a head!

Reach into my pocket, find betting slip;
take it out angrily, give it a rip!

A day at the races? Stay away from the courses.
I've lost all my money on backing slow horses!

## St. Swithin's Day

Don't cause the rain on St. Swithin's Day,
with misery and with lies.

Don't cause the rain on St. Swithin's Day,
and curse me to darkened skies.

Bring instead the sunshine, friend
with laughter and joyful ways.

Bring instead the sunshine, friend
and forty balmy days.

## **Good Buddy**

What do you look for in your friends?
Perhaps it's brains or money.
What do you look for in your friends?
Someone who is really funny?

What do you look for in your friends?
Some only have one rule:
That they should have enormous hands,
to catch you when you fall.

# Just Some More Poems for Everyday People

## Book 2

# Jon Palmer

# For Mo..........

Inspirational, irreplaceable.

*I hope that you like them, Mum!*

© 2016 Jon Palmer

## Sssshh!

Ssssshh! Do not speak,
there's nothing you have to say.
Let's sail through swinging barley
and stroll through swathes of hay.
Let's squint our eyes at azure-blessed skies
that makes good this summer's day.
Let's thrive in golden silence
and wander far away.

## A Walk to Coate

Remember that walk out to Coate?
Sauntering steps through the ancient path
cut deep into the coombe and deep into history
banked high
the sun unseen behind
making its presence felt on exposed necks
and on pale open shoulders

Remember that walk out in August?
We steadily clambered the ever steepening way
that had begun to bleach the turf through pounding feet
we lightly touched the tough textured teasels and felt their
solidity
as we passed by
carefully side-stepping cow carved divots
that sought to trip the unwary

We walked on to where the oaks spread
and the brambles brazened
to where goldcrests skipped effortlessly
from twig to branch to limb

We heard little as little distracted the ear
only the soft tramp of children
and laughter, and whistle and song

The land spoke in chords
the water tinkled hers
time banished almost to irrelevance
being was all that mattered


Remember the path that was
ransacked and ramshackle through the nettles?
It had offered no hindrance to our travel
and the redundant brick red bridge
that once catapulted travellers
over the downs and off to the city
or the seaside
but now sat immobile and hidden
from the eyes it once served
visible only through errant shrub and shunting willow herb


Musk mallow and foxgloves were not shied
by our presence
but welcomed us in vivid hues
of purples and pinks
Coate would soon be before us
singular in near silence
or a-bustle with the flush of crowds

It mattered not....
either would be fine

## Elixir

When you are tired, rundown
or rather a little stale;
nothing revitalises you better
than a pint of strong ale


## A Cheesy Poem

I had a terrifying nightmare,
at my age it's silly;
it wasn't my fault,
it was the Caerphilly


## The Dreaded Munchies

I've got the late night munchies,
it's making me rather crazy;
somebody's got to help
and fetch a chicken jalfrezi


## An Indian Diet

You won't lose weight on this diet,
in fact, your get more largy.
Go easy on the naans, my friend
and have just the one onion bhaji.

# We're All Going On a……

We are going on summer holiday,
will you pack your bags with me?
We're going on our holiday,
who will be the first to see the sea?


Let's build a sandcastle with bucket and spade,
spend all our change down at the arcade,
fly a kite and watch it soar,
catch a wave on a body-board.
Explore rock-pools with a net,
watch the weather forecast, sun or wet?
Cast a line with baited hook,
become engrossed in a fantastic book.


We are going on summer holiday,
will you pack your bags with me?
We're going on our holiday,
who will be the first to see the sea?


Shall we throw that jack, have a game of bowls?
Then crazy golf, eighteen holes?
A game of football, two-a-side?
An afternoon donkey ride?
Go off crabbing on just a whim?
Brave the cold ocean and have a swim?

No, let's flatten the sand to make a wicket
and enjoy a game of fab beach cricket!

Shall we sit in the evening sun, just talking?
Or take to the promenade for walking?
How about somewhere peaceful, not too loud?
Or people watch the madding crowd?
Browse the shops and with the masses mingle?
Have a dance upon the shingle?
Relish a pint in 'The Rose and Crown'?
Or savour an ice-cream as the sun goes down?

We are going on summer holiday,
will you pack your bags with me?
We're going on our holiday,
who will be the first to see the sea?

## Graffiti

The writing was on the wall
and I was a fool
and ignored it.


The writing was on the wall
but I strained tall,
too proud to believe it.


The writing was on the wall
yet I stooped small,
too cowardly to face it.


The writing is on the wall
it is harsh and it is cruel,
believe, I must, I wrote it.

## ....Say No More

Give me a nudge,
tip me a wink;
maybe I'll swim
or maybe I'll sink.


Wheeling and dealing,
ducking and diving;
I'm just some geezer
having a go at surviving.


## Life on the Front Row

I love the physicality of sport
but honestly see no fun
in being gouged and bitten
bound in the front of the scrum.

Ouch!

## Dungeoness

I strained to look up from my dungeon
through iron barred
windows
that narrowed my view
to a mere piece of a
jigsaw
I pulled at the chains
that held me
the harder I heaved
the greater the resistance
resistance felt futile

I sank to the floor
and sat, wearied


I was forced to take that moment
to pause
to stop

Looking once again at that
restrained view
I watched the clouds pass by
one by one
slowly, quickly
billowy, dreamily
moving to their will
guided by an unseen rhythm
at liberty in the blueness

The prison window widened

The sun began to warm my face
the warmth swelled in intensity
growing in body and in mind
stealthily and steadily
the chains
melted
link by link
they unfurled and fell to the ground

I leapt-up to pull at the confining window bars
hungry to see more
but there was no need for my haste
for the bars, like the chains,
were gone
the vista was clear

Calm transcended to me
worry descended from me
the jigsaw lay completed
that rarest of things came to me
peace
I was a free man

## Never Let That Picture Fade

I will never let that picture fade
or gather thick with dust,
for to gaze upon it every day
will forever remain a must.


My memories may wax and wane
but that photo will help to muster
treasured images of yesteryear;
it shall never lose its lustre.


To keep your picture, is to keep you here
and forever is a must.
I will never let that picture fade
or gather thick with dust.

## To The Doers

Feed your esteem, enjoy your spoils!
Yes you, the façade fakers.
For you are but a folly;
you are the tiresome takers.


Honour to your toils!
Yes you, the dedicated doers.
You are but legend;
you are the difference makers.

# Discovering Your Family Tree

I am off to trace my family tree.
Will I find fortune or illegitimacy?

Will I discover palaces and manors abound?
How great does a title and heraldry sound?

But what if it's a notorious villain with an infamous face?
A story from abroad, a far-flung place?

Maybe a musician or a company director;
a fantastic idea from an eccentric inventor?

The call of war, a march to the drum;
a rustic hovel or London slum?

A working man, a suffragette;
carpenter's chisel, fisherman's net?

Workhouse rules, endless wealth;
national fame or blighted health?

Rural landlord, factory floor;
other side of the country or just next door?

Nomadic lifestyle, life-long loyalty;
surely not? Really? Royalty!

What has been I cannot change,
but it matters not you see.

For it doesn't make you any better,
or any worse than me.

I am off to trace my family tree.
Will I find fortune or illegitimacy?
I am off to trace my family tree.
Oh, the fascination of ancestry!

## Blinkered

I rode across the city today,
siting in the back of a cab.
Me and that taxi driver,
engaged in a lengthy confab.


We looked through our frosted experiences
and put this world to right.
We gave our strong, damning opinions;
we spoke through our tired, tainted sight.


I may be sat in the same seat
as so many with differing views
but what gives me the right to denounce them
when I have not walked in their shoes.


## For the Love of Lardy....er, Hardy

A glass of apples, dappled shade,
a slice of Wiltshire lardy
and two lazy hours, dreamt away,
with a book by Thomas Hardy.

## The Flicks

Friday night and what could be more groovy
than a bag of popcorn and a thrilling movie?

## ....Only In My Mind

I'm down on the dance floor
but my moves, they revolt her.
A few beers later
and I'm the new Travolta!

## Blimey

Goodness me, that really stunk!
In a former life, were you a skunk?

## **Firestarter, Firewalker**

We are not the pyro-obsessive,
the warped starter of the fires.
We are not the hate-ridden bellows,
whose words fan the flames ever higher.

We are not the gullible accelerant,
who fed on others and gorged.
We are not the egotistical crucible,
where jealousy is forged.

We are the firewalkers,
we tred the burning coals,
we can walk on your fires
and absorb them with our soul.

## An Old Birthday Card

I traced each word you'd written,
followed each letter with my finger.
I allowed myself to drift away
and that digit to pause and linger.


The ink still fresh, the paper bright,
it was as if yesterday,
that you had scribed those very words
and had your little say.


I do not care about lavish belongings
or the big deeds people do.
Thank goodness for the little things;
for they bring me close to you.

# Wonderment

An object of wonder, a thing of beauty;
will give the spirit a raise.

Yet such magnificence; may pale and pass
and astound for only days.

So in my mind, I'll bag it up,
and to a safe place, I will send.

Then I can reach in at any time
and it will never end.

# Maelstrom

The person stood, silent, and peered unbalanced into the void
and an impenetrable and eternal blackness stared black.
The person stood, quietly, and teetered by the edge;
frightened, they leant away but felt the void pull them back.


The person shut out the pain, the movement, the constant noise
but they were weakened and the void knew and dragged them along.
The person was a fighter and tough and they resisted the gravity
but the void was encompassing in its depravity, and grew strong.


Battling wildly with their thoughts, the person fought with all they had
to stay strong; with resilience, belief, and foundation
but Pandora's Box had begun to open;
the destroyer of sanity and of salvation.


Nightmares and demons ravaged in the confusion.
Every vanquished memory that ought
to be imprisoned, revelled in its freedom,
then overwhelmed; they were caught.

Turmoil! A soul destitute, how the devil tormented,
ridiculed, riddled, mocked and fed.
Chaos is no ally, no friend;
this is a half-life, perdition. They felt better off dead.


The maelstrom was the shroud the person wore,
it constricted and left them destitute to that dark abyss, and they fell,
silently screaming into that that tumultuous nothing,
in desperation, the person reached out an arm to avoid this hell....


They tumbled in circles of vulnerability and distress.


A hand grabbed back, a semi-helpless limbo,
the person swayed, heavy in the ether and heavier in their heart.
Eternity passed, they held on.
A tiny glimpse of hope, the foreboding began to part.

## A Christmas Carol

The church door
a millennium in age
rough, textured, weathered
as to be irresistible to the touch
gently opens
a small breath of winter enters
flickering the candles
flames dance in brave opposition
to the blackness
looming outside

The light and the shadows
move  to its rhythm

To the very corners of the cross
swept the light
making the unseen, seen
the vague, clear
momentarily
picking out faces
fresh, glowing
excited, worn
before extinguishing them from view

then pausing

on the thick stone walls
to reveal the craftsmanship
of the mason and of the carpenter


The light lent elegance
beauty
serenity
holiness
crisp yet soft
natural and temporal
a lesson in itself


A shared inhalation
a shared moment of community
carols fill the air
sung with honesty
equally by all
it mattered not that the notes were not exemplary
things, in isolation, rarely are
but together, as one whole,
that rare thing….perfection.

# The Blessed Sprite

I whispered to the tree sprite,
"I apologise for the deforestation."
She whispered back,
"The word, I think you'll find,
is devastation."


I said to the tree sprite,
"I am so sad for your loss and distress."
The tree sprite said back,
"And they call this progress?"


I shouted to the tree sprite
"How can I make them listen?
This is all for money and gain."
The tree sprite shouted in response,
"It's a world gone insane."


I screamed out to the tree sprite,
"I am so sorry, this is wrong!"
But no response came back again,
for the tree sprite, she was gone.

## The Wreckers

Almost was I vanquished,
consumed by the torrent sea;
when high on the cliffs above
you held a lantern for me.


In the nadir of the trough, I lost it,
blinded by looming crest
with every zenith rise, I saw it,
beacon of the tempest.


How that candle fuelled my hope,
and called and did implore;
through malicious, troubled waters,
and guided me to shore.


I tumbled onto the beach,
battered, torn but safe;
weakened by tribulation,
mangled was my faith.

From the higher ground you came down
and you took me by the hand,
you had rescued me from spiralling currents,
and now led me to safer land

Then when, finally, calm blew the western winds,
life turned again and mocks;
you swept me off my feet
then dashed me on the rocks.

## Footprints

Exacting memories may slowly fade
like footprints in the sand,
but the feelings that they evoke
shall endure and always stand.

## Never Forget

Never forget and never doubt
how you brighten all my days,
with that enlightening smile
and all your little ways.

## Katy - Ode to the Cider Apple

Wassail! Wassail! Where will I find her?
Cheering and jeering and drinking the cider.

Sing her a song and sing to the breeze,
praise to the orchard and praise to the trees.

Thank for the harvest, now sleep and now rest
return in the spring, my friend of the press.


## Poppadum Pals

What a woeful world,
if we can't sit and stare
and have some poppadums to share.


## A Great Plan

The 'jobs to do' are mounting.
"They are doing in my head."
I don't know where to begin,
so I'm going off to bed!

# For Our Alfred

There's company in solitude,
a host of chattering thoughts.
It may not be company to you but it's a fine company of sorts.


There's company in solitude,
humble, honoured hours.
Whereas solitude in company,
both derelicts and sours.


The joy of thought, of learning, growing,
the love of nature, discovery and knowing,
the joy of finding, in every hollow,
something new or old to follow.


There's company in solitude,
a host of chattering thoughts.
It may not be company to you but it's a fine company of sorts.


**For Alfred Williams (1877 - 1930) - 'The Hammerman Poet'**

*Hope you found it, Alfred, or, at least, are still enjoying looking!*

# Further Poems for Everyday People

## Book 3

Jon Palmer

Simply for
Kerry, Sam, William and Daisy

©Jon Palmer December 2016

## A Breath of Heaven

I was asleep,
I had been sleeping for years;
a slave to my worries,
my failures, my fears

I was asleep,
out cold on my feet;
nothing was cohesive,
nothing complete

I was asleep,
rarely awoken;
worry and mundanity,
shackles unbroken

Moribund, shattered,
close to my death;
when the wind struck my face,
a heaven's breath

A breath of heaven,

a joining of dots;

I'd been asleep,

now I was not

## It Seems Ages Since I Last Saw You

It seems ages since I last saw you

When we walked barefoot on the sand

Making footprints and then smiled and were buoyed

As they faded and flattened as the sea filled the void


It seems ages since I last saw you

When we journeyed to the pond

Taking stale bread and ripping it with our fingers

As we fed the ducks and together just lingered


It seems ages since I last heard you

When we listened to the game

Sat with a cuppa around the wireless

As we chatted and listened unitedly tireless


It seems ages since I last saw you

When we went out for a drive

Just viewing things we pass from the car

Destination irrelevant, not travelling far

It seems ages since I last saw you

Now I have few reasons to go

And all is so wrong;

No more little big things

Since you have been gone

It seems ages since I last saw you

## Murmuration

As the summer began to give a delicate sense

of making its gradual but inevitable friendship with autumn

yet, arguably, was still deep and wonderful

once was glorious with golden crop

harvested now

yet now glorious again

in vivid blues, oranges or red skies

that illuminated the evening

that could so completely astound

and make the heart bound

unbeatable

almost unbeatable

then comes the murmuration

the dance of the starlings

so ordinary it sounds

so florid the show

so innocuous in individuality

so indelible in mass

It ripples, rolls

and twists on itself

through the sky, dominating the sky

dervishesque

in vigour, verve and vitality

it spins again and again

wraps neatly inwards

explodes outwards

billows

unfolds

swirls

twirls

the light flickers with it

whirls

and skims

and fades and glows

embellished parade sweeps as it flows

rhythms in greyscale

flamboyant fanfare

Myself, transfixed to the spot

My eyes, transformed to the heavens

As a school child,

we experimented in lessons

with iron fillings and a magnet

made them stand then fall again

reel and turn to our instruction

at our total command

no-one commanded here

I was a spectator in all this

Glad indeed, pure bliss

## Chance Encounter

If we meet

aged and old

will we greet

with tales told

will we speak

of chances blown

or will we seek

to defend our own


choices listed

speak in tongues

mistakes twisted

of when we were young

thoughtful smile

good deed and sin

sit a while

soak it in

## **Concussed**

I was concussed

in the confusion

of the chaotic consternation

caused by

the collapsing

of the cosmic constellation.

Crikey!

Catastrophe!

## Standing on a Long Barrow

If you ever find yourself heading west
out on the M4 or the A4 and before
the chance passes you by
search out the Marlborough Downs
those chalk-lands of antiquity

Stand on the feat which is West Kennet Long Barrow
see the fields roll away before you
in all directions
billowing in huge dips and rises
as if blown by some prehistoric wind
waves of an terra sea

Look under your feet,
to that ancient barrow
its size and substance
and ask yourself why?
did this mighty task of earth shifting
and stone lifting

become the tradition and who?
is so honoured and so respected
to be buried in such a noble spot.

Look to the skies
to the movement of the clouds
to the migrations of the birds
look to the north-west
and ask yourself what?
reasons, still an enigma, made
them raise Silbury Hill from the ground
sometimes moated, always round
Ever impressive

Then bring your focus a little closer,
along the same line
buried from sight
by shrub and fall and hedgerow fine
Swallowhead Spring
Mother of the Kennet
Grandmother of the Thames
sometimes resting, always alive

Sacred, hidden
Folklore bidden

In all directions
no matter whence you came and where?
you are heading
or when?
you are here in the rotations of the year
Openness
Freedom


The M4 and A4 may beckon but before
take the time to savour the elements, feel how?
the sun gently heats the skin and warms your heart,
and find
the wind breezes through your hair
and ruffles your mind

## Go Large

I have earned it and I have the salary,
blow dieting and counting each calorie;
I'm going large

My stomach is greater than even my eyes,
so please do not skimp on those golden fries,
and make that burger in a bun,
the biggest you can, a massive one.
I'm going large

I drawl at the dream that is gherkins and relish,
the mere thought of it all is something to cherish,
and how about a drink, what can you make?
Yes madam, I'll have the biggest milkshake.
I'm going large

Hey, I'm only human, it's not my fault;

I simply have a craving for lots of salt.

And how about a side to make it zing,

I'll take an extra portion of onion rings.

# I'm going large

I'm lovin' the food, soon I'll be back,

that is if I can avoid a heart attack.

# I'm going large......for now anyway

## Lost in Translation

I spoke my heart

In silence and screams

As we drifted apart

In a desert of dreams

The opening of lesions

The first blood you drew

Tried to find reasons

When reasons were few

Chillness envelopes

Coldness hanging

Melancholy develops

A cymbal clanging

In translation lost

In isolation weep

Warmth turns to frost

Embitters my sleep

Shiver in thought

Radiance gone

Normality sort

Playing our song

It's hard to forget

Harder to forgive

Lost in translation

A half-life I live


Laughter and alliance

Rapidly fade

Still seek reliance

Black turns the shade

I am comatose, I am inert

Hopelessness my elation

Constant my hurt

Damned in translation

Face in the dirt

Complete denudation

All is so curt

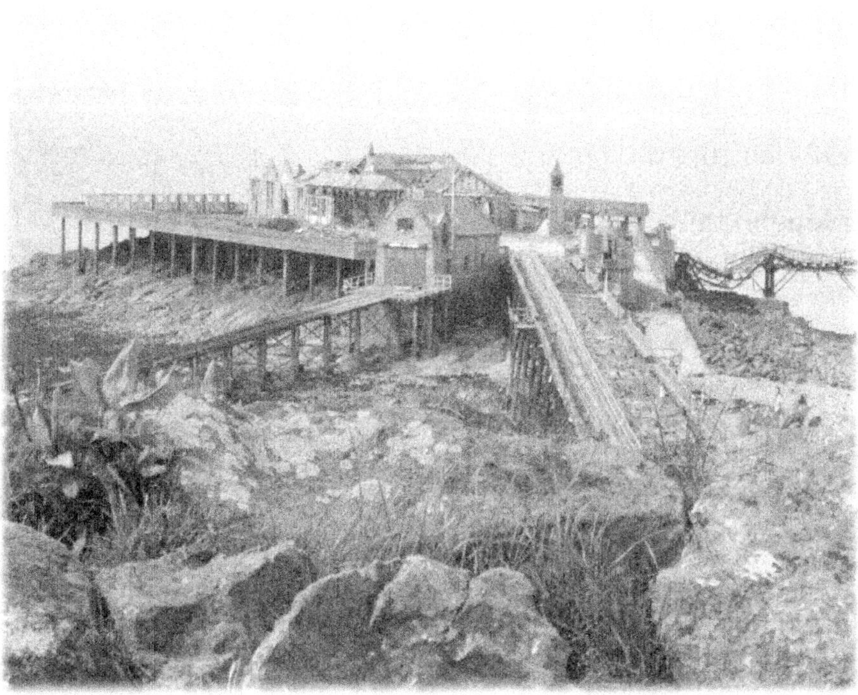

## The Church Door

I ran my hand across
the rich furrowed grain
ploughed not planed
and by centuries stained

Rougher than the hands
that made it and scythe
paid for in toil
the burden of tithe

Dried now by
a millennium's breath
witness to jubilation
and feelings bereft

Entrenched within
those emotions felt
held in undulation
lowness and stout

The more I feel

the more I grasp

there is such wonder

in touching this rasp

# Autumn Fire

I took the embers from a thousand fires

and threw them to the breeze,

watched in open wonder

as they settled in the trees

and glowed as bright as ever before

as a myriad of flaming leaves

Then on winter's days, when all is grey

and cold and dank and dire,

I'll warm myself once again

in the thought of those blazing fires

## A Monday Wish

Please hear my plea:

Help me to get out of bed

With this tired head

Out of the black and into the red

Please make:

The working hours fast, leisure time slow

Hassle less, wages grow

Boss happy, traffic flow

I also politely ask:

To finish on time, breaks for tea

Pay for overtime, a rise for me

Little hassle, life stress free

And, please, also:

Keep those printers online, full of toners

Help me rise above the haters and the moaners,

Complaining customers and constant groaners

Indeed:

Keep the phone lines open, computers working

Sickness away, workmates from shirking

Fat bloke in the warehouse prevented from twerking

Yet above all of this:

Help support the needy

Placate the greedy

And make Friday come rather speedy

Bless us all....everyone!

# Abandoned Quarry

Rock strewn dusk
  full with fern
    of uneven undulation
      and layered strata
        of twisted vine
          and snaking water

Dark rutted path
  potted with footprint
    under deep canopy
      with dog rose garter
        nature's solidity
          and human martyr

Work winds the way
  through steepened rock face
    disfigured by hammer
      by son and daughter
        nature's fragility
          and human slaughter

# **Moonlight**

Moonlight
Soft moonlight
Reflective, un-defective moonlight
To this time alight

Alight upon the ocean
Give sight upon this place
Play upon the rippling tide
And rest upon your face

Dance amongst the shadows
Walk where no-one dare
Stay with me this dark night
In love, in hope, in care

## The Rare Hoar Frost

Hoar frost's sugar coated masterpiece delivered
Rousing the soul when bodies shivered

Inanimacy encouraged
Iced detail clarity
Winters rare gift
Appreciated charity

Focused intimacy
Of each reed, each web, each singular stem
Pure white on off-white
Fog in the fen

How fabulous the freeze
Admire its work
Aesthetic magnificence
On contour lurk

## But for The Grace of God go I

Biting December

hungry and cold

a tramp rummages the bins

"It's a penance," I'm told, "for all his sins."

He sleeps alone

in isolation outside

his headboard, a stark concrete wall

"It's all he deserves," I hear, "stupid fool."

His trousers threadbare

shoes worn

jacket almost in tatters

"Stay away from him," they say, "that's all that matters."

His hair is brittle and matted

filthy skin

"Social excrement, human rat"

They decree "Well, whose fault is that?"

Eroded by the battle for survival

he tires, he falters

feels no prospect, has little hope

They shout, "Have you no self-respect, you dope!"

Christmas Day

no change, no cheer, no presents to untie,

no rum, no roast, no festive mince pie

"There but for the grace of God go I."

## The Naturist

Some people love it,
some think it rude;
to stroll about freely
and all in the nude.

Some wish to try it,
I'm not that bold;
I'd be rather embarrassed
and extremely cold.

## The Chicken or the Egg

What came first
the egg or the chicken?
It's a fifty-fifty bet,
so which are you pickin'?

# Walk from the Station

The rain emptied the streets
and cleared my mind
solitary amongst myself and my thoughts
alone amongst the solidity of the terraces
alone in the starless evening

I felt alien from the nesting hordes
who were now enclosed, warming their bodies
in front of their fires
and their well-being in a cascade of TV, tea and toast

I realised in an instant that
I was back in the streets I had walked
so often
hand in hand
as a child

I took a breath
the moisture-rich air filled my lungs
the rain almost fragrant

and its coldness felt readily on hands and cheeks

The occasional street lights
brightly mirrored
in the puddles
made more stark by the contrasting
blackness of the road
sparkled the surrounding darkness
to a gleaming shiver

My mind danced with it
hurrying me back
to those childhood days
splashings of salt and vinegar
on freshly fried chips
strangely aromatic
a heavenly antidote to
damp hair and a chilly
November evening after
an evening swim at
the local red bricked baths
built in Victorian philanthropy

warm, filling, homely, honest

I heard the voices of
friends and family
clear
familiar, fun, carefree
close enough
real enough
to answer
to almost touch

The voices continued
as I walked
to resound within my head
It was great to hear them all again
snippets of time
supposedly ephemeral
but hibernating among my daily thoughts
sleeping, just sleeping
waiting to be stirred by the
tiniest spark to the senses
wonderful, just wonderful

A car sped by

splashing a puddle

and waking me from my dream

it had been a fine dream

I was comforted and contented

I will go there again some day

Soon

## With My Blessing

I made a wish, a simple wish,
    and cast it to the skies

It caught the wind, a gentle wind,
    and off it took and flies

Through the blue, the fulsome blue,
    and up and through the clouds

Above the Earth, this bewildering Earth,
    beyond terrestrial shrouds

Be free my wish, this simple wish,
    to a haven, safe to rest

Then in that place, some sacred place,
    be heard, be felt, be blessed

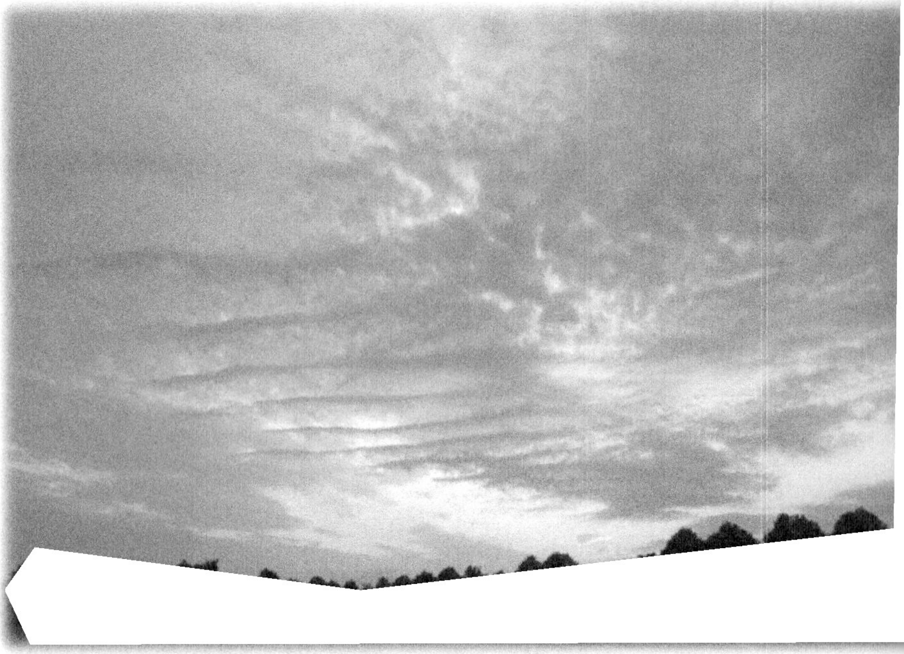

## The Green Man

Hold the power, Green Man
Hold onto the light
Through the darkness of our winter
Keep it safe and bright

Release the power, Green Man
Let the sparkle flow
In the dawning of the spring
Let the magic grow

Show the power, Green Man
Let's glory in the sight
In the bounty of the summer
Reach the zeniths' height

# On Widcombe Hill

On Widcombe Hill, tall stand I
Above minutes and hours, here to fly
The golden stone alight below
Across meadowed carpet
In splendour glow

Our time is but short, temporary lent
Amongst these heights, 'tis time well spent
The golden stone faced below
In meandering coombes
In majesty glow

A pause earned, a juncture flavoured
Faith regained in this moment savoured
The golden stone noble below
Across berried hedgerow
In brilliance glow

On Widcombe Hill, tall stand I

Above minutes and hours, here to fly

The golden stone elegant below

In Minerva's care

In eternal glow

## A Theft

If fate was a thief

and stole my sight and my hearing,

I could still enter a room

and, without ever fearing,

I'd know you were here,

just the same,

and through the twilight,

I'd cry out your name

## Your Majesty

I am in awe

pure awe

raw awe

I felt, I smelt

I saw


Your Majesty

Mesmeric!


Ancient pendunculate oak

fairytale, melodramatic tree

honoured to be here

albeit humbly

aside


Your Majesty

Mesmeric!


So primitive, so striking

slowly waning, ever strong

gnarled and immense

respected so long


Common, not common

so far from this removed


I am honoured, I am blessed

so exemplar

so more regal than the rest


I am in awe

pure awe

raw awe

I felt, I smelt

I saw


Your Majesty

I bow to your greatness


Mesmeric!

# Unbroken Circle

Man distrusts

Respect slows

Man divides

Hatred grows

Contempt swarms, humanity goes

Man unleashes untold woes

## At the Crossroads

Meet me at the crossroads, dear
Meet me there tonight
Meet me at the crossroads, dear
Let's choose the path that's right

When good times were prevalent
And fun and laughter ruled
We chose the road correctly
We were never fooled

Then tough times reared their ugly head
And sadness filled the skies
We chose the path correctly
Together we were wise

When disaster struck with an iron fist
And caused our ship to list
We stumbled along the road correctly
Through storms and grief and mist

Now more sane times, perhaps are trundling in,

Or so I hope I'm right

Meet me at the crossroads, dear

Let's take the path that's right

# Up on the shoulder of the Giant's Grave

The Vale of Pewsey before me splayed
As if by holy hand were laid
Greens by every hue and shade
Weaved and twined, divinely made

Who else could have placed every tree
Juxtaposed so perfectly?
To blend in such a worthy show,
Patchwork stitching by hedgerow

Man placed his homes within this land;
Humble cottage, manor grand
By chance or by plan? All I can say,
Is that it augments this medley in every way

A train hyphenates through, appears and gone
On the ear, a mistle thrush song
Smoke rises from distant fire
Elevates the church's spire
And for the nose, a rose's scent
Surely, somehow, all this was meant?

This morning's prize grows and ever yields,

Further views across fine fields

The glory of each hue and shade

Here eternal, never fade

As here I sit and here I stayed

The Vale of Pewsey before me splayed

# The Side Street Side-step

The oppressive crowd began to take their toll;
then the side street side-step saved my soul

To gaze upon empty slab and stone;
distant now the tiresome drone

From hum and hassle and swirling shoal;
the side street side-step saved my soul

Lichen looms and railings rust,
carved stone, plaques, and window dust
a hidden gem - a real plus
observant eye - a valued must
delicious detail not frantic fuss


From hum and hassle and swirling shoal;
the side street side-step saved my soul

# The Road to Perdition

I walked the road to perdition
Cursed but never bowed
I faced the wrath of damnation
Determined, never cowed

You can burn me in your inferno
And slate my name in vain
Never will I surrender
Through hurt or hate or pain

You can batter, you can scorn
Cast me out asunder
I am here, here I stand
Impervious to your thunder

I walked the road to perdition
Potted, winding, long
I looked square into the eyes of damnation
For I had done no wrong

# Flag of Convenience

I sailed under a flag of convenience,
through high sea and tempestuous gale;
kept it flying so visibly
when the trade winds faltered to fail

I sailed under a flag of convenience,
through peace and through raging war;
I never nailed my colours to the mast
for I am a cowardly fool

## Up on the Ridgeway

Hawthorn, blackthorn, path-worn green
Through England's chalklands, millennia seen
Walked and ran, rode and trodden
Pathway through our nation, never forgotten

Hornbeam, whitebeam, path-worn green
Defensive hill-fort, beacon seen
Summer burn, winter frost
Pathway through history, never lost

Hawthorn, blackthorn, path-worn green
Coombe and copse in custody seen
Pastoral brilliance, liberty pure
Start and end, never quite sure

Hornbeam, whitebeam, path-worn green
For future millennia please be seen
Remove from my boot, a claggy clod
Look to the hills, respectful nod

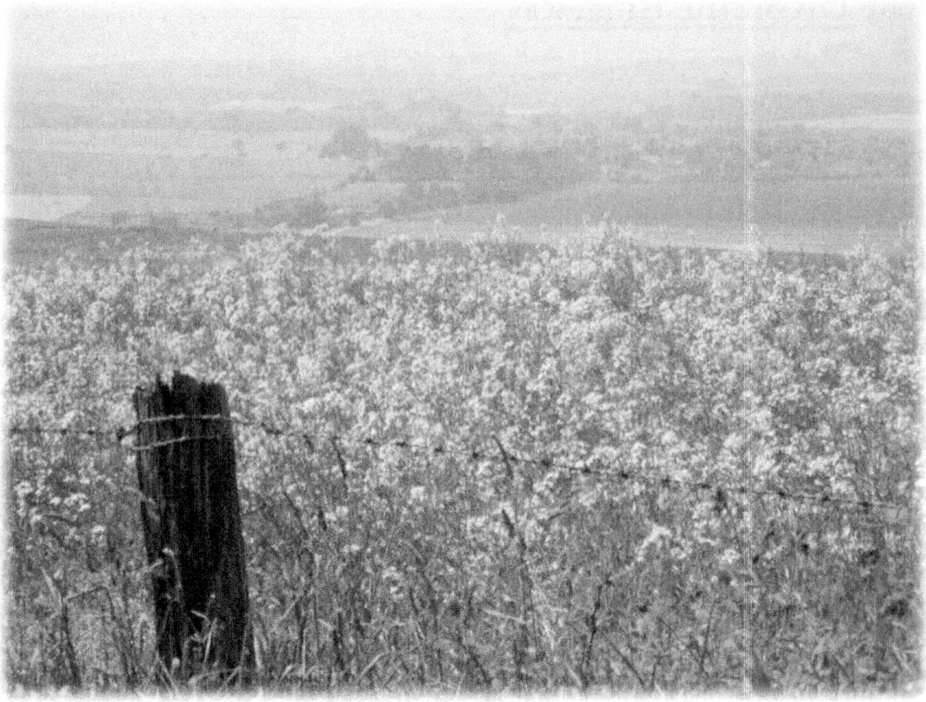

# The Laughter of the Ha-ha

How the ha-ha laughed
    in mocking tones of red and green
Out of grasp
    yet so clearly seen
 Lay the Promised Land

In mocking tones of green and red
"Look, don't touch!"
    the ha-ha said
Out of reach
    yet so clearly seen
 Lay the Promised Land

Oh, how the ha-ha jeered to deride
Tormenting my soul,
    and bruising my pride
Beyond touch
    yet so clearly seen
 Lay the Promised Land

A vision of what could be

A vista clear for all to see

A dream pictured there for me

The ha-ha invites so temptingly

And lays before the Promised Land

# Driving the Porcelain Bus

Saturday night, out on the town,
the cider I'm supping,
got a thirst for the apples,
the ale I'm snubbing

The magic of 'trampagne',
the drink of the gods,
bitter-sweet nectar,
I'll give it the nod

Thirst quenching liquid,
a taste bud delight,
perfectly matured,
for an eventful night

But heed this warning,
make no fuss,
seven pints of scrumpy,
means the porcelain bus!

## Mrs. Chiropractor

Hey Mrs. Chiropractor,
bend me back into shape.
I want to be vertical,
not some twisted ape.

My head does not turn,
I can't look to the right.
My shoulder is frozen,
my muscles tight.

Everything aches,
I can only dream of bending.
This sciatica is killing me,
the pain's never ending.

I loathe this condition,
I feel one hundred and two.
So Mrs. Chiropractor,
just do what you do!

Warp me, snap me,
flex me double;
use your wisdom
to end this trouble.

Click me, flick me;
just do it today
and align correctly
each vertebrate.

Untrap any nerves
or just lesson their grab.
I promise to exercise my core
and firm-up my abs.

I'll lift correctly,
my knees I will bend.
I won't slouch when I sit,
I'll make posture my friend.

I will not complain when
your fees don't get smaller;
if you can make me pain-free
and one inch taller.

So Mrs. Chiropractor,
bend me please into shape.
I want to be vertical,
not some twisted ape.

# Bench over Porthmeor

I sat

legs tired from the climb up the steepening hill

legs wearied by the day

and by the long year

I gazed

at the panorama

before me

The beach

wide, expansive

book-ended

by rocky headlands

was largely empty now

Empty of the emmets

who busied and burnt themselves

in the full heat of day

playing in the sand and rockpools

or unbusied themselves

bathing in the sea and the sun

and now elsewhere at their want

in hotel rooms, restaurants,

pubs and promenades

Just a few souls now ventured

onto the evening beach

dotted here and there

sporadic

walking, talking, observing

becoming extras on the scene

before me

Waves still crashed

and thundered

magical

their white crests visible

even from here

but now free from the compounding hordes

in swimsuits and shorts

that earlier

interrupted their flow

and made shabbier their beauty

in the name of amusement

but that is fine

absolutely

although

I am biased

as I was among this

fun-seeking, madding crowd

Returning to the present

I shut my eyes

the waves still slapped

and slammed

into the sand

the unrelenting force

carrying even to me

blinded

way up on the high ground

I waited here

unusually

for a long time

sublime splendour and tranquillity

foes in my entrapment

Slowly

my eyes opened and drew to the foreground

silhouetted gravestones

numbering in their hundreds

but seemingly more

many more

lay

at a symphony of angles

shapes, shadows, angels

Sons and daughters

of this town, this brine

who lived and loved here

who must have seen this vista

time and time and time again.

Did they ever tire of it?

How could they possibly?

And now they
viewed for eternity
its tides and moods
its rage, its calm
always its beauty
always its magnificence

I thought back to personal memories
of time spent in this place
great times, great people

This pausing
had distracted me
I had not been aware of the sun
burning orange, pure inferno
as it progressed across the sky

It appeared to move slowly
at first
but then
in illusion
much more quickly

dropping

sinking

beyond sea and soft sand

beyond craggy cliff

out of sight and sound

Positively humbled

I felt rather miniscule under the power of nature

my fate in all this vastness

unknown perhaps,

perhaps

ultimately decided elsewhere

Was that a bad thing?

One last look

across the headstones

and the headlands

one last deep inhalation

of breath and smell and memory

and I was gone

# IT Luddite

I admit my ignorance, my luddite ways
but I simply struggle with every craze.
I am not scared to say that my energy saps,
at the thought of gadgetry and each new app.

I care not for Microsoft, Facebook or Apple,
to me it is all something confounding to grapple.
I might be a sceptic; maybe I'm around the bend,
but those tiresome emails are too easy to send.

And what at those people left all bereft
by anonymous trolling and cyber theft.
And what do I do when my identity goes missing,
just because some fool is doing some phishing.

I admit my ignorance, my luddite ways;
I know I'm a fool to ignore the next phase.
Yet I am willing to say, and I hold-up my hands,
the internet can be amazing on super broadband.

And I can sometimes see the incredibility in IT and tech

and I....., oh what the heck,

it's me, I'm a fuddie, I want to go back

especially now my laptops been hacked!

## Pointless

Do not think I am laughing,

this is a manic smirk;

the truth is I am floundering in all the paperwork.

The printer is exhausted,

my pen is running dry;

there are reams of A4 foolscap stacking way up high.

I have arranged it rather neatly,

putting it in pile upon pile upon pile;

so that it can be filed forever in some obscure and forgotten file.

Maybe, one special day,

it may all be read;

before somebody decides to end it all with a final shred.

Do not think I am laughing,

this is an angry smirk;

the truth is that I am sick of the waste that is pointless paperwork.

## Just Nice Words

I adore the sound of elbow,

of rollicking and red rose,

RAF Brize Norton, RNAS Culdrose.

How about halcyon, serendipity, and 'be cuddled',

breakfast, bootleg, bamboozling, batty and befuddled.

Wander down Watling Street, weep on Wembley Way,

trample on the Trussocks, cruise on Cardigan Bay.

Durdle Door for dancing, bike out to Banbury Cross,

go crazy in Ogbourne Maizey, wonder Wye in Ross.

Holiday in Mevagissy, Mablethorpe, Westward Ho!

Perhaps the Roseland Peninsula is just the place to go?

Climb upon The Kymin, Long Mynd or Cader Idris,

pass up through Achnamara, picnic down in Bliss.

I adore the sound of concoction,

castellation and far flung;

how they dance within my mouth

and roll across the tongue.

# The Edwardian Photograph

Who are you, young lady?
What was your fate?
Immortalised splendidly;
forever in nitrate.

Did the dice roll kindly?
The cards fall your way?
Were your hopes all answered?
Did good luck hold sway?

Were you a kind soul, successful,
harridan or friend?
Was life for you a blessing
and fulfilling to the end?

# Those Night-time Hours

Rejuvenated not quite redeemed

Hope implicit in all thee dreamed

Cathartic, so it seemed

At thought in those dark night hours

At thought in those dark night hours

Funicular be the dalliance

Contentment be in salience

Trespass abide in transience

Serenity in those dark night hours

Cathartic, so it seemed

## Caught Between.......

What of the future?
What can you foresee?
Caught between the devil
and the deep, blue sea

What of the future?
What will it be?
That fathomless ocean
and the devil delving free

## Bar Stool

Never is a tale
So tall or so far
As that emanating from
A stool at the end of a bar

# A Glass Half Full

My glass is half empty

Fill it up, mate

Give us a good top-up

I'm quite in a state

A lift, a bunk

A helping hand

A beacon in the shifting sand

My glass is half empty

Fill it up, mate

Give us a good top-up

It's getting quite late

A helping hand

A bunk, a lift

A bridge across a cavernous rift

My glass is half empty

Fill it up, mate

Give us a good top-up

I'm up against fate


A helping hand

A lift, a bunk

Sensibility in the ceaseless junk


Thank you, bless you

A kind thing to do


My glass is halfway to full

Fill it up, mate

Give us a good top-up

I'm feeling just great

## Ode to the Sprinter

### Usain Bolt

To call him less than a great
would be an insult,
to the lovable talisman,
that's Usain Bolt.

A tropical storm,
speed without fault;
Is he human,
this Jamaican Colt?

### Michael Johnson

Sharper than a razor
made by Ronson;
I bow to your greatness,
Michael Johnson.

## Jessica Ennis

I'm glad she took up athletics
and was just average at tennis.
Hurrah for the fabulous
Jessica Ennis.

She got better with age;
what a thrill!
The multiple talents
Of Dame Ennis-Hill.


## Flo Jo

Not even her nails
could make her slow;
what a loss,
the great Flo Jo.

## Christophe Lemaitre

I peered out of

mon fenêtre.

A blur, Mon Dieu!

Christophe Lemaitre.


## Tyson Gay

He wishes he was born

in different era, a different day;

though he is still rapid,

poor Tyson Gay.


## Allan Wells

So quick through the air

his tartan swells;

the 80s McSpeedster,

Allan Wells.

## Veronica Campbell-Brown

Such power per inch
in this Jamaican Japonica;
the mightily gifted
and astounding Veronica.

## Allyson Felix

Fast and graceful,
she's on racing slicks;
one of America's finest,
Allyson Felix.

## Spirit in the Words

There is a spirit in these woods
That thrives within this place
That lives amongst the flora
With resilience, strength and grace

Resides in matted bramble
In incising, intruding thorns
Throughout even the heaving shade
The spirit never mourns

Through fallen bough, choking ivy
Under stooping bower long
Even in foreboding crevice
The spirit still is strong

And as the light fights its way
At the edges of the glade
The spirit grows more abundant here
Wood melick, sedge and blade

And in the glade its very self
Where canopy is lean
Great mullein and foxglove
Their poisonous beauty seen

Beyond still the spirit glorifies
In the wider clearings and open ride
Sweet violet, knapweed, pimpernel
and countless cousins grow beside

Hear the Nightingale's
Churring jug jug tune,
Fritillary in fecundity
Butterflies bloom

There is a spirit in these woods
That thrives within this place
That lives amongst the flora
With resilience, strength and grace

There is a spirit in these woods

That thrives within this place

It lives within myself too

And all the human race

# Illuminador

Scepticism in ascendency, belief on the wane
Slate ridden skies of sleeting rain
Perspective losing, accelerating insanity
Balance the contradiction, rage the disparity

The darkest second precedes the dawn
Hope springs eternal where hope can be born

You shone a light for me when no-one else dare
Believed me a path with credible care

I owe so much, too late I discern
Belated thanks, can only return

You shone a light for me when no-one dare
Illuminador – unending in prayer

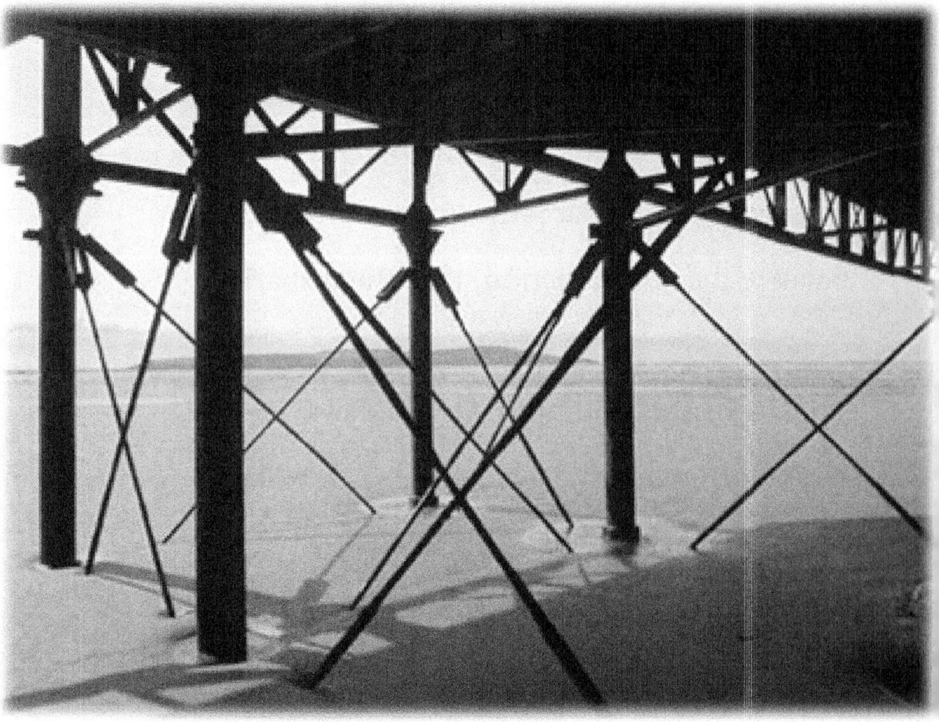

## The Giggle

Keep the zest, go even dafter

Rejoice in the sound of untamed laughter!

## The Town Crier

Oyez! Oyez!

Learn ye! Learn Ye!

It is not all about the destination;

it's also about the journey!

Printed in Great Britain
by Amazon